OSGOOD

OSGOOD

Deborah Allbritain

Brick Road Poetry Press
www.brickroadpoetrypress.com

Copyright © 2024 by Deborah Allbritain

Author photo: © 2024 by Deborah Allbritain

Library of Congress Control Number:
ISBN: 978-1-950739-12-7

Published by Brick Road Poetry Press
314 Lee Road 553
Phenix City, AL 36867
www.brickroadpoetrypress.com

Brick Road logo by Dwight New

ALL RIGHTS RESERVED
Printed in the United States of America

To the people of Osgood

Table of Contents

Depot..........3
The Jewelers..........5
The Neighbors Across the Way..........7
The Twins..........9
The Tuffin Sisters..........11
Obituary: The Widow Kessler..........13
The Lost Ones..........15
Rupert..........17
Lilla May..........19
Little People..........21
Tilly..........23
Manly Debeck..........25
The Uncles..........27
Addison..........29
The Tall Man..........31
Manly..........33
Nikanor..........35
The Academy..........37
The Great Aunts..........39
Mr. Woolsey..........41
The Silences..........43
Addison..........45
Diana of the Dunes..........47
Oscar..........49
Mila..........51
Bread Baby..........53
The Dive..........55
Harriet..........57
Eben..........59
Cake..........61
Charlotte..........63
Abbessa Elena Fevronia..........65
Mrs. Reed's Boarding House, South Bend..........67
Aunt Ida..........69
Ghost People..........71
Hubbard Squash..........73
Horace..........75
Saffron and Sage..........77
William Fading..........79
Lena..........81
Arthur Doe..........83
Ours..........85
Laddie..........87

Hattie	89
Me	91
The Graveyard	93
Mr. and Mrs.	95
Abide	97
My Mother	99

Depot

Summers, we'd run barefoot down the hill from our house, watch ice blocks unloaded from boxcars. Sawdust. Wagons.

Hiss of pistons, the throttle nudged another notch. Pennies on the track.

Run until we were outrun. Farms and more farms and berry fields. Milkweed and bluestem oceans.

The only way in and the only way out. Platform of sending off and welcoming home.

The shriek climbing frigid nights, and the plunge back into darkness. Ghost faces.

Before you could even turn around, the frames of the film are gone.

Even if there is no one left to tell our stories. A dusty box of photographs passed down and down. Maybe there is that.

Have faith, pray Darling, things will have a way of working themselves out.
Because everything arrives and everything leaves.

The Jewelers

William Fink was revered as the best jeweler in Ripley County, despite the fact that he was the *only* jeweler this side of Versailles. Mother said that the Finks had more money than the whole town of Osgood put together. I envied their daughter Millicent who on Saturdays, lollygagged in the shop with her mother while I cleaned the chicken coop. I'd have given my eye teeth to sit on that velvet-plush stool working the cash register.

At least that's what I thought until the day of the robbery. One Saturday, Mr. Fink had gone fishing with the men from the Angler's Club, when a stranger flew through the shop's door yelling *this is a hold up,* and fired two shots, one of which hit Millicent in the knee.

The Ellinghaus twins claimed to have witnessed a man with a dark moustache racing across the street pushing a baby carriage. They said he was the spitting image of John Dillinger but turned out it was the preacher's nephew escaped from the asylum. And the headless baby, just a doll with a removable head, perfect for stuffing jewels in.

The whole experience took a toll on Millicent who from then on was confined to a wicker wheelchair. Mr. Fink took to liquor and soon after, Millicent's mother died of consumption.

Satan preys upon the vulnerable, my mother declared, *and he always leaves behind a sign.*

And then I remembered the headless baby.

The Neighbors Across the Way

Sometimes they stood on the peak, staring out. Sometimes they sat on the gable, feet dangling. People had different theories as to the reason. Our teacher said we had overactive imaginations and that no one in their sound mind would recite scripture or fly kites from their roof tops.

My mother thought the man meant well and was merely teaching his children bravery. *After all*, she said, *they don't have a mother.* My grandfather speculated that not only were they closer to the breath of God, but they could also spot the wall clouds and green sky of a tornado.

The day I summoned enough courage to cross the road and ask the man myself, I pulled the bell and waited. Through the peep hole, an empty room—except for a ladder and three sets of wings collapsed on the floor like fallen doves. Come spring, we heard from the postman

that the family had moved into the widow's cottage on Barnum Pond. The boy developed such a fear of heights, he had stopped growing. And his sister, with her luminous hair, claimed her name was no longer Luella, but Seraphina.

We all prayed that by living closer to the ground, the children might have a chance at reaching full potential. When I got older and couldn't sleep, I would gaze out my dormer window looking, waiting for something, but not sure what—only that it was possible.

The Twins

Whenever there was trouble in Osgood, Ed and Cecil were there along with Dolly, their beloved chestnut. Whether it was the day the horse trolly ran offtrack and crashed into the drug store and

they risked their lives pulling out the injured, or the day Nikanor got lost in Manly's orchard, the twins appeared like two rumpled angels.

If you asked where they lived, you never got a straight answer. Ed would point east. Cecil would say *just north of here*. If you tried to follow them like my little brother often did, Dolly would

refuse to take another step and you would be kindly told to go home. Once, just after a new snow, my brother was bound and determined to track them as they headed home through the

forest. As it was getting darker and colder, out of breath and caked in snow, he banged through the kitchen door. *I saw them* he wheezed, *I saw Ed and Cecil change into two white eagles, and*

Dolly turned so white, she even had wings. My mother sent him to bed with a cup of Ovaltine and a ham sandwich. The next morning at breakfast we asked him what happened in the woods.

I was almost frozen to death, I don't remember a cotton-picking thing.

The Tuffin Sisters

After their husbands died, Mary moved into Caroline's home on Beech Street where they conducted seances on Saturday evenings. Sometimes the sisters would allow Horace and I to join around the kitchen table because we had *unobstructed vibrations*.

Their ability to communicate with the departed, they maintained, was a result of spending every summer at the Chesterfield Spiritualist Camp. *We owe everything to the gifted Madame Carrièrre*, one of them would sigh. Madame apparently was known for producing ectoplasm from a number of orifices. Caroline said it looked like *a smokey extract unfurling from her lips*. Horace speculated it was more likely regurgitated cut-outs from the French magazine *Le Miroir*.

And it was Horace who finally proved the sisters to be fakes. One Saturday, with the lamp turned to a flicker, the séance began. Horace sat next to Mary with their hands joined and legs slightly touching, so that Horace could sense any manipulation of props.

When Mary's feet started to jerk Horace lunged for the lamp in the middle of the table, turned it on high illuminating Mary holding a Y-shaped wooden handle fitted with two white gloves.

Those are no ghostly hands, he hollered.

Horace you goddamned son of a bitch, Caroline screamed. *Get the hell out of here and never come back.* By the time we got home we'd laughed so hard our ribs were on fire.

Why aren't you wearing your glasses, I asked.

I am, he said, *aren't I?*

Obituary: The Widow Kessler

On May 2nd, The Widow Tess Leader Kessler succumbed to our Lord Jesus Christ. The Widow is survived by her brother, Corning Evening Leader, a Methodist clergyman from

Indianapolis and the Widow's beloved goat, Enoch II, (who The Widow claimed was the reincarnation of her late husband, Enoch Bond Kessler).

Enoch II, attired in a cut-away morning coat and trousers, designed by The Widow personally, was said to have remained at her bedside until The Rev. Leader arrived to perform the last rites.

The Widow has bequeathed her estate to the care of Enoch II, whose spirit she believed, was akin to the Divine. The Rev. Leader concurred that Enoch II "seemed to be instinctively

religious," and went on to say that his "Christian character continues to shine with untarnished luster, even though my sister Tess has been called into the Kingdom of Heaven."

The woman was around the bend, my father whistled, *simply around the bend*.

All my brother and I could think of was how to rescue that poor goat.

The Lost Ones

None of them knew how to swim and the only kid that claimed to have seen them that day, drowned in the spring freshet in 1902. There was something dark about the river, something

more than its cold brackish muck. My mother called it *the devil's river*, and if she knew I had snuck out every full moon that summer, that there were six of us with broomsticks who
    prodded

and tapped our way along the bank looking for corpses, she would have had a fit to end all fits. We never told how we discovered Billy's boy scout ring and his mother's sunhat gleaming in the

runoff. How we carried our lanterns into the forest and buried them together under the birches. How we slid back through our bedroom windows and into our beds with our clothes on,

wondering if we should tell our parents, wondering if something terrible would happen if we
    did
or didn't. For example, Billy showing up at our doors in his boy scout uniform, and saluting.

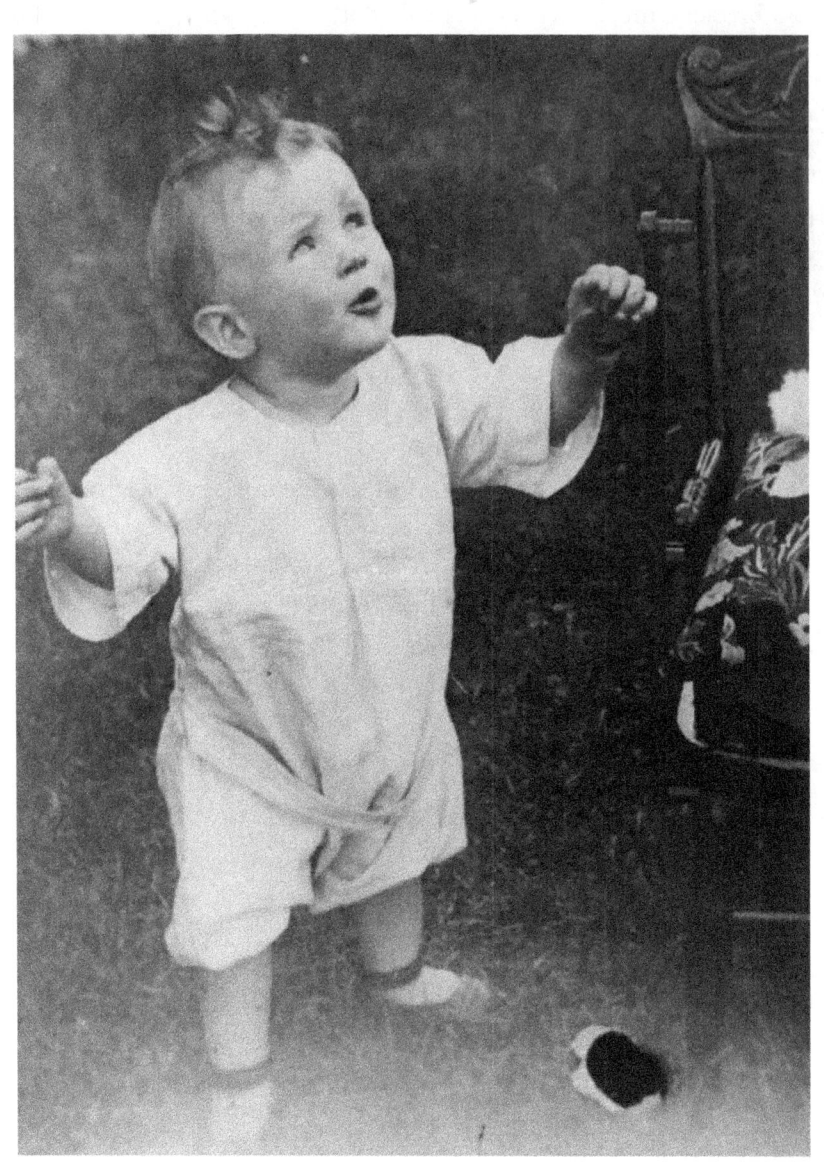

Rupert

The summer my older brother Rupert turned sixteen, he and my parents rode the train to the Shelbyville Chautaqua at Eagle Lake. They said my little brother and I were too young for revival meetings—that seeing people crying and carrying on would give us night sweats. Grandpa said that Rupert always had *the calling*. Even when he was small, he'd lift his arms toward the heavens speaking gibberish. Grandpa said Rupert was talking to Jesus, but Aunt Leota said it was more likely he'd just soiled himself.

My mother's letters told about how Rupert took to camp life like a fish to water—ushering folks to the mourner's bench, lighting the camp torches, even handing out the eucharist for conversions. She said some nights when the sermon and lamenting got folks whipped into a frenzy, they'd send Rupert up to sing Be Still Thy Soul of Mine. On Repentance Fridays, the reverends put him in charge of tallying up the collection plates, but if they knew my brother the way I did, they would have had second thoughts—

Near summer's end Mother wrote that Rupert would be staying on full time with the Chautaqua. Time past and we had no word from him until that day a card arrived with no return address. Inside was a lock of hair and a note that read:

Rupert, God rest his soul, was the only man I have every truly loved. May the Lord comfort you in your time of need… Sister Elizabeth Rose

Lilla May

There was something about Osgood that caused forgetting. Take the little house in the middle of the forest that my mother claimed had been abandoned for years. Horace and I wondered

whether to tell that a very tall, old woman lived under its roof. But only in summer. My mother said Lilla May was a figment of my imagination which made me wonder which one of us was of

sound mind and which one of us had a screw loose. Horace said it was the ghost of his grandmother because she wore the same kind of wool socks and never smiled, but as time

progressed, we both agreed she was the spitting image of Willa Cather's mother. Once I peeked through the kitchen window and noticed a white apron hung over the drying rack, a surplus of

books, and a miniature teapot. Another time, Horace said when he peeked, Willa Cather's mother was fastening a diaper onto a baby pig. *Are you sure it was a pig,* I asked?

A human baby would never oink, he cried.

In winter, we'd hike through snowdrifts for hours, trying to remember where the house had been but besides some frozen pea vines and brown geraniums, all we could see was our own breath.

Although I couldn't swear to it.

Little People

In summer we spent most of our waking hours trying to get away from little brothers and little sisters. Even when our parents put us in charge, we only pretended to watch them. Sometimes one would wander off in the woods and not be found until a day or two later. I think our parents

thought of us more like dogs or cats which could never be counted on to do as they were told. After the summer Billy disappeared somewhere down river, people started to pay more attention to the consequences of giving us older kids free reign. But even when curfews were instated, we

found a way around them unless, as often happened, a little brother or sister would rat us out. Luckily for me, my brother was a late talker and when he did finally start, it was in Romani. My Grandfather said that sometimes gypsy blood gets passed down the generations.

The little sisters were the worst snitches. And the only way we could keep them quiet was with bribery. Bribery and self-sacrifice. If they complied, we played whatever they wanted. Folks would stare in disbelief as we dressed baby dolls, braided hair, even pretended to be horses.

Horses that tossed their heads in the wind, that reared and galloped through the pasture, enduring the jabs of small feet in their ribs, knowing that freedom was coming.
And it never came soon enough.

Tilly

The summer my cousin Tilly returned from New York with a handsome new wardrobe, was when my mother told me the hard truth, that not everyone ordered clothing from the Sears catalogue. And that was the beginning of the great divide. While we girls rode horses through the jack pines of Indiana, ditching our siblings or trying to drown Horace in the swimming hole,

Tilly gallivanted around in her new straw hat, which could easily have been mistaken for a side dish. We teased her something terrible until she'd scream: *Don't you poor girls know anything about society, this is my coming out year for heaven's sake!* Nobody knew what she would be coming out of—Millicent thought it had something to do with Lister's towels and the Hoosier

Sanitary Belt. But then in December, there was a photograph in the Osgood Journal of Tillie and ten other girls lined up on the stairs at the mayor's house wearing white ball gowns and holding tiny bouquets. I didn't know what to make of it until I showed my mother—*The only respectable career for a woman is marriage*, she said, *and the best marriages are made by debutantes.*

It was then that I realized the whole thing was a trick. And Tillie, though she couldn't have known it at the time, would outlive three husbands, which probably contributed to her death, as well as drinking too much of her antidote for melancholia, a prescribed mixture of laudanum and gin.

Manly Debeck

Mudpie was the most prolific sow in the county. To say that we were tripping over ourselves in piglets every spring was an understatement.

When the fair came to town one summer, my little brother wanted to enter the "America's Fastest Swine" racing contest. My grandfather said the popcorn eating might be a more fitting enterprise, since my brother already knew how to do that.

I'm signing us up, my brother shouted, *Mud-Mud Junior and I are going to win.*

The training took nearly three weeks, dozens of doughnuts and the expertise of Manly Debeck who lived two farms away and could teach a pig to do almost anything.

She's faster than green grass through a goose, Manly laughed.

On the day of the contest, it rained buckets. The piggies and flying mud, the squeals when they ended up in a roiling heap, was more than my brother could take.

What a shame, my mother crooned, wiping his cheeks with a handkerchief. *No need to fuss,* Manly told him, *let's go spit some cherries, maybe enter the Mr. Legs contest.*

In my brother's arms Mud-Mud's pink lidded eyes crinkled shut with sleep. *Poor piggy, you gave it your all,* said Manly, *let's get you home and into bed with some Ovaltine,*

and with unwavering affection, gave him a smooch on the snout.

The Uncles

The first spring after Millicent came to live with us was when Uncle Royal and Uncle Jack arrived from South Bend in a red Pierce-Arrow. They were on their way to Detroit where Royal said the big money was and they pinched our cheeks until they nearly bruised.

My mother referred to her brothers as good-for-nothing fops and the fact that they arrived hours late, only proved her point. Once, I asked if they owned a steel factory or one of the railroads, but she said no, that their money likely came from gambling or something equally

untoward. But we loved our uncles, not only because they brought the most beautiful ribbons and hair combs, but because they possessed a more raucous spirit than any grownups we knew. *C'mon family, time for hide and seek in the privet hedge*, and after supper, *Everyone in the*

parlor for charades. Millicent and I fell asleep that night in a drowsy-sweet haze of hubbub and tobacco smoke. Next morning, both cots were empty. And as I wheeled Millicent in her chair to the kitchen and asked where they were, my father just said *gone*.

Millicent started to wail, and I ran outside hoping the Pierce-Arrow would still be parked alongside the barn, but all that remained were tire tracks and a run over cigar. As to the disappearance of my father's corn knife, axe and two shovels—

Nobody likes to be made a fool of my father said and spat on the steps.
And I held the cigar deep in my pocket, that later I would touch to my lips.

Addison

If we weren't swimming the river we were up in the fort, two boards shimmied between the V of an oak.

We liked the sensation of being dirty. Skin powdered with dirt or bee pollen. Blackberry-stained mouths.

I loved her in a way I knew was unsaintly.
Beers and cigarettes. Liquid tongues.

Curls pushed away with the back of my hand.
It was July.

The Tall Man

He often appeared in photographs. Some thought he might be a buttonhole relative of Lilla May's; others, like my grandfather, claimed not to see him at all. Whenever someone would ask "but who is that tall man?" whether it be in a photograph album or incidental snapshot, my grandfather said they needed spectacles. My little brother swore he saw the tall man at the circus

once, but it turned out to be a funambulist balancing on a low wire. Around Christmas time when the tall man showed up in an advertisement for Tea Rum, my grandfather hollered: *by George, if he isn't the spitting image of that sod from Boston who succumbed to the Great Molasses Flood.*

Impossible, I thought—on the other hand—molasses and rum, rum and molasses, it almost made sense, in an Osgood sort of way. But if you asked me about it then—the photographs, whether

I saw him or not, just to be on the safe side I would hedge, because even when some things are right in front of you, they can't be trusted.

Manly

It started with the scavenger hunt. No boundaries. Ten o'clock curtains. Home base the old pecan tree in Manly Debeck's orchard.

I had collected every item on the list that night, all except for the boot hook, and hearing voices coming from Manly's summer cottage, I figured it couldn't hurt to ask.

From a part in the curtain, I could see Manly on the divan beside Mr. Woolsey, the bespoke tailor on Buckeye Street. Manly held a sleeping piglet while twisting a snuff-colored strand of Mr. Woolsey's hair between two fingers. I knew it was a sin, but when Mr. Woolsey leaned over

and kissed Manly, they looked as if they'd been painted onto a screen—the flushed faces, dark suits, two glasses of sherry and the little pig, the one Manly had taught to blow kisses.

No matter how hard I tried I could not look away.

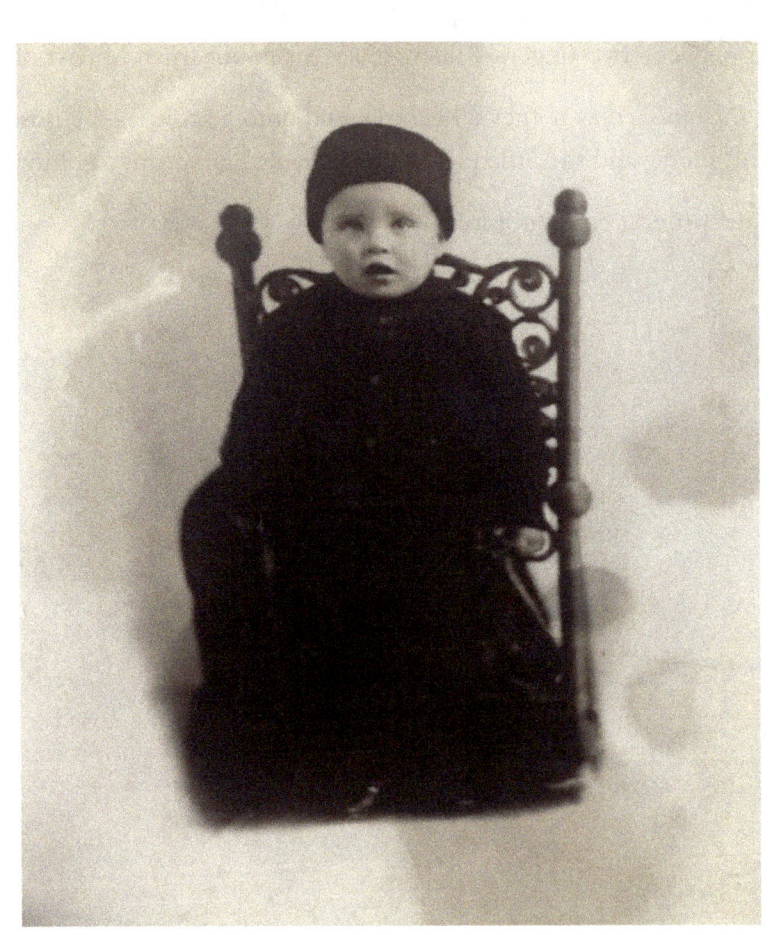

Nikanor

It was snowing when we found him sitting on the steps where Lilla May's house appeared during summers. His blue lips, his eyelashes laden with snow crumbs. "Bolsheviks," he whimpered, then pointing to his chest,

"Menya zovut Nikanor."

Horace and I took turns carrying him out of the woods, and by the time we plunked him onto the kitchen table he was sound asleep.

When my grandfather moseyed in from the bedroom, the boy shouted "dedushka, dedushka!"

That's Russian for grandpa!

We unbuttoned the heavy brocade and stitched inside the lining were five brooches, four sapphire bracelets, an emerald necklace, and a place setting for twelve.

The Academy

My mother said I was lucky to attend Osgood Academy, that many children didn't have the opportunity—but except for music class and history, I could have done without it, especially sewing and mending.

However, because I was a model student, I received special privileges like sitting in the front near master's desk and the stove, instead of in the back rows where the troublemakers shivered through the morning.

Master regularly held up my sheet of Spencerian script as an example of precision and quickness of thought. In the morning when fingernails were checked, I got to distribute the toothpicks to those whose nails were unacceptable.

And the fact that I was class president, gave me clout and a confidence that I was above all disciplinary measures—until that afternoon they heard about Addy and me—Naturally,

we were as shocked as anyone. Straightforwardly, we denied everything.

The Great Aunts

My mother says I should not be afraid when Great Aunt Hannah and Great Aunt Edith yell in German over who makes the best sour kraut and schnitzel. Whenever I do speak up

which they always tell me, *speak up dear*, Great Aunt Hannah says I should hold my tongue so I can learn something but all I've learned is how to slide under the long dining table like a real

ghost which maybe I am anyway, and curl up around the billowy clouds of skirts, wait for someone to say: *There must be a little mouse tickling my feet, I wonder where our little darling has gone.*

If I don't come out this minute and finish supper, my father will get the hickory stick like the time I got caught peeking through a crack in the outhouse door and saw Great Aunt Edith

sipping from a tiny bottle that looked like rosewater, but my mother said it was special medicine. After I said my prayers that night, she rubbed my backside with salve and reminded me that

if I spy on grown-ups, I should never ever tell what I'd seen.

Mr. Woolsey

He was as handsome as Prince Albert of Belgium and had a slight stammer which the smart-aleck boys mimicked behind his back. *He needs a wife,* my mother would say, *a well-turned man like Mr. Woolsey, unlike most of the men in Osgood who refuse donning even a spritz of Florida Water, should have no trouble.*

Woolsey and his shop reek like the underbelly of a musk-deer, my father opined.

Addison said Mr. Woolsey drenched himself in Fougère Royale, which reminded her of heliotrope and roses after the rain, with top notes of clary sage and base notes of tonka bean and oakmoss. Addison knew her herbs.

And we both knew we would forever be in his debt, and he in ours. It was Mr. Woolsey who came upon Addy and me in the tall grasses behind the school yard. *We're done for,* I sobbed into her mussed-up hair. *I trust him and so should you,* she avowed.

Not only did he never rat us out, the next time we saw Mr. Woolsey who was English and versed in Shakespeare, raised his boater and sputtered *m-mum's the word girls, m-m-mum's the word*. He gave a little wave and winked, which we were never sure was a wink, or just another endearing tic.

The Silences

Fishing was something we did to humor my mother.

Go fishing today with your father, talk to him, she'd say, but my father preferred silences.

Silence between us and him, silence between one catch and the next, silence broken only by the burgle of the creek or some yellow rumped warbler in the pines.

I told my mother she should come see for herself how talking, at least to children, and fishing, were not his idea of sanctity. Still, she would plead, *talk to your father, ask him about his trophies, go out on the porch and tell him what you did in school today.*

But it was always the same, my father staring off at something we could never see, something more satisfying than whatever it was we had tried to give.

Mother, we'll do the washing up and you go talk to him.

Ask him why he sits so long on the riverbank watching us.

Addison

We didn't know if there were any girls like us, but we knew we wouldn't find them in Osgood. Moving to South Bend after graduation was my idea and Addison had agreed, up until Uncle

Jack's younger brother came to visit. *New York George,* Jack called him, with his dark curls and stylish frame, sold ladies' apparel to the best shops on Fifth Avenue.

After dinner one night, George opened his two sample cases and adorned Addison and me in bolero jackets, crepe-de-chine tea gowns, scarves, sailor hats, lace blouses, and buckles.

All of our dresses are mounted with the softest of linings, for to rustle, my dears, there is no longer desire, George informed. I flushed with all the attention, but Addison, who had been a debutante, must have seen her chance.

She was charming, coquettish even, the way she held her hand out for George to kiss— Unbeknown to me, it was a family set up, another hijinks, ambush of the heart—those late afternoons of kisses, our legs vining over the faded counterpane, doomed.

My mother said I had best grow up too, find an eligible gentleman to marry, *like Addy would.* I settled on Vassar instead. But always, I spent summers back home working the farm, riding horses with my little brother who was now taller than all of us.

Some nights when it was too hot in my room, I'd walk through the woods, climb up into the old tree fort. I still heard Addison's whisper: *If you could have one wish, what would it be?*

I would wish to be your husband.

Diana of the Dunes

According to the Osgood Journal:

"Cleaving the water like a milk white dolphin came a mermaid. She made the shallows, rose up out of the water, then like a fabled nymph, flitted off into the shadows."

The fact is, said my brother, *Alice Mabel Gray, was a real person who gave up her wage-earning life in favor of living in a windowless driftwood shack like a hermit. Why a lady with a college education would want a life of berry picking and solitude is beyond me!*

What's more, fools who travel to the Indiana Dunes because they think Mabel's ghost might run naked down the shore and disappear into the water, couldn't tell a skunk from a house cat! My Lord, don't they know a myth when they hear it? Diana of the Dunes!

It says right here: "Alice Mabel Gray's life ended tragically after her husband, wanted by the law, beat her senseless after the birth of their second child. And that is the sad truth, period."

My mother, wringing her hands, wondered what had become of the children.

Without thinking I jabbered: *Oh, the girls are with Diana,* which only caused my brother to mock: *I suppose that time we camped at the dunes you turned yourself into a dolphin and splashed about with the lot of them?*

Only the daughters, I replied.

And they both laughed.

Oscar

After his father died, Oscar, being the oldest, was expected to provide for four brothers and sisters plus his mother, who as far as we could tell, did little more than complain about being

a poor widow, and all she got from the Lord was a broken spirit. Millicent said it was Oscar's spirit that was breaking—Delivering ice in the early morning hours and in the evenings, stacking

shelves at the grocer's. At school he got smacked with the cane for falling asleep, which Millicent believed she could have prevented had she been able to sit in a desk instead of her wheelchair.

If only I could sit behind him, she'd say, *nudge his shoulder when he started to slump*. On weekends my father found Oscar extra work around the farm and my mother always sent him home

with a pie. Nobody knew he was saving that money for the future and nobody but me knew he and Millicent were in love. Perhaps it was the wisp of hair that curled in front of his right eye

or the fact that he was so strong he could run with her on his back and never fall. Or maybe it was because he didn't see the wheelchair at all. And maybe instead of his mother's

disappointment, *Oscar, you cannot make a silk purse out of a sow's ear,* when he finally proposed to Millicent, he heard those three words that had never been said to him. Ever.

Mila

Turns out Nikki was not a Romanov, the jewels were glass, and after a few months we began to wonder if anyone would claim him. She appeared out of nowhere, with a fox tippet cascading

off her shoulder and a knitted cloche pulled low as if she were expecting snow in June. *Mila,* she said, *Nikanor mama*—We stuffed Nikki's things into mother's worn carpet bag,

along with some fried chicken and half a cherry pie. They left on the night train bound for Cincinnati. The events of that day spinning like a horse spooked in a night meadow.

My father wondered if we should have asked to see her papers or some kind of proof. My grandfather shook his head. *Blood knows blood when it sees it.*

Bread Baby

Oscar acted as if it was normal to receive a baby gifted to him out of the blue. The note, pinned to the baby's left sleeve read, *For Oscar and Millicent, no inquiries, no returns.*

It arrived on the pullman during one of the worst snowstorms in the history of Osgood. She was a healthy baby with dimpled cheeks the color of a Parson's Pink China rose, and although

she came without instructions, caring for her was no different than if she had been a newborn lamb. The only difference being that she preferred sleeping inside the bread drawer. Millicent

and Oscar began every cold morning with prayers of gratitude, ending with the words

Give us this day our daily bread baby. Curled around a cozy loaf of potato bread reminds her of her ancestors, Millicent maintained,

ancestors and wild yeast.

The Dive

Turns out George's business went belly up, and what she thought was love, was only pretense.

When she came back to Osgood looking for me, I had already moved to South Bend and when I picked her up at the station, nothing had changed, because that kind of love doesn't wane, it just gets boarded up in the heart.

Maybe there is something about Osgood that causes forgetting, but in South Bend it all came back. It came back in spades.

Harriet

Maybe Oscar knew their time together would be cut short.

If he wasn't building her a dollhouse, he'd be teaching her to ride the pony. If she wasn't sitting on his lap driving the tractor, she was snuggled between him and Millicent on the porch swing every night.

If she wasn't riding on his back, she was handing him tools from the shed. If he wasn't pushing her on the rope swing singing, *Harriet Harriet swinging so high, riding in her chariot ten feet*

high, he'd be teaching her how to plant seeds in the garden. And if she wasn't climbing him like a tree, she was slung over his shoulder like a flour sack.

When the fever started the night of her fourth birthday the doctor said it was probably due to sunburn and over excitement. But Oscar knew there had already been over a hundred cases of

scarlet fever that summer and several deaths, news he did his best to keep secret from Millicent. Harriet's fever raged eight days and her breathing grew difficult before it stopped altogether.

God give us this day our daily bread baby oh Lord and save us who are crushed in spirit. Amen.

And we prayed for God's chariot to take their beloved girl home.

Eben

Eben wrote his first poem at age four and at the age of eight, he published a batch of elephant poems in The Indianapolis Star. He found school crushingly dull. Even with being accelerated, he knew more than any other kid, and often, his own teachers.

But Eben was quickly becoming an outcast, preferring adult conversation to what he called *baby games*. *What's to be done about Eben?* his mother would lament, *he is a heedless genius, oh what's to be done?*

It was Eben who brought up the traveling circus, saying he'd like nothing more than to travel with the elephants. He figured he could create his own act, reciting Shakespearian sonnets, Longfellow, maybe throw in some of his own elephant poems.

Forget it Eben, no son of mine is going to be a circus act, yelled his father, *end of discussion.*

But Eben never forgot and when he was old enough, he got in with Barnum and Bailey and became the sensation known as *Child Genius*.

I am happy, he wrote home to his parents, *and finally I have a best friend.* He didn't mention it was the most famous member of the circus.

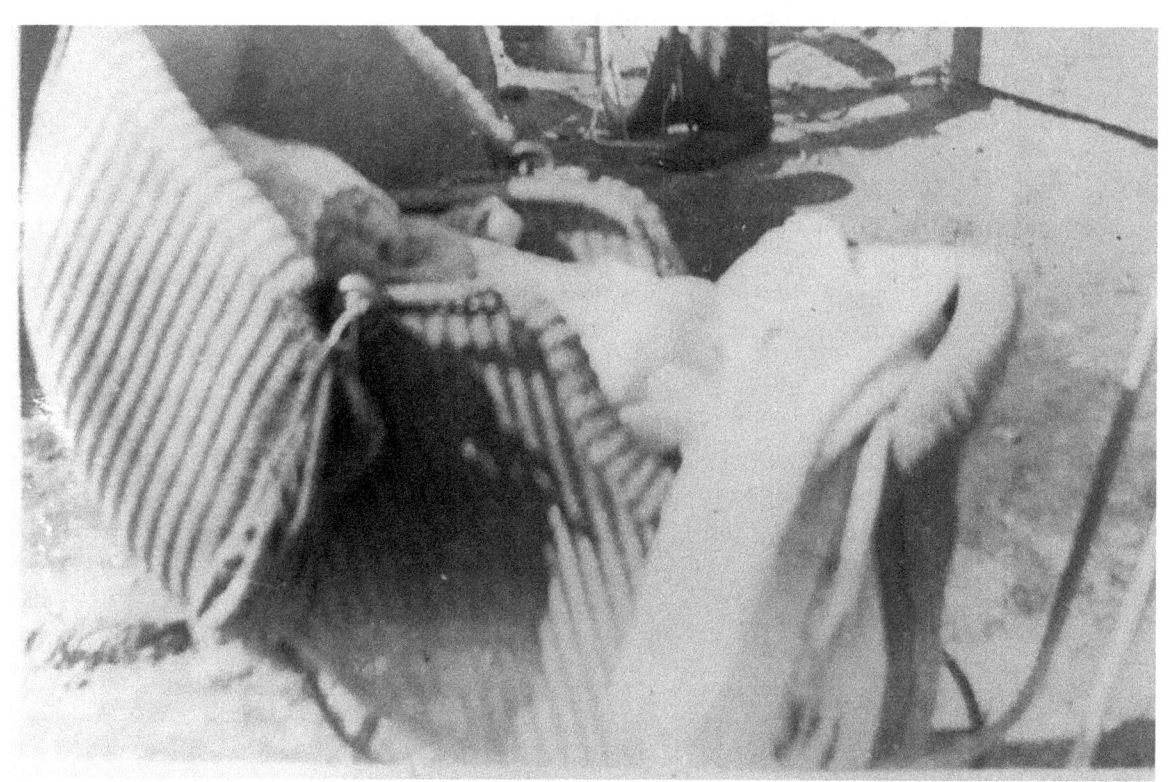

Cake

She couldn't get enough—pound cake, nut cake, coffee cake, jelly cake.
Most mornings she'd be up to her neck in Gold Medal Flour. It wasn't until

Oscar took her to the doctor that the suspicions of some became the joy of us all:
Millicent was going to have a baby. Her own baby.

We celebrated that evening with biscuits and gravy followed by Millicent's famous
pineapple upside down cake.

After getting the children tucked in, I collapsed into bed, Horace reaching around me
pulling me close, his worn-beautiful hand falling onto my wrist.

So many blessings I thought, giving in to sleep, glorious sleep—And the dreams
blossomed out of control, unstoppable, abiding dreams
of Addison.

Charlotte

Manly Debeck's mother, who having left the sanctity of marriage, for the fleeting passion of a sailor, ended up spending her last years in the asylum, whereby, according to the records, she died of delirium.

Some folks said it was guilt and the wallowing tendency of her poems that drove her mad. *What is the point of going on*, she'd write, *Satan and men have destroyed my life*.

For years she had tried to prove to Manly's father that she could be trusted again, even swearing on a bible and the preserved bedsheet her own mother died on, but he insisted that Charlotte was *just one more betrayal* in a long line of betrayals that began in his childhood.

Mr. Debeck preferred the company of his floor to ceiling collections which we'd heard included: toy fire engines, wristwatches, back scratchers, Merck & Company coffee tins, and wagon wheels.

What finally pushed Charlotte over the edge was not only delirium, my mother said, but Manly's loving attachment not to his own mother, but to Mr. Woolsy, the bespoke tailor.

You cannot drink the cup of the Lord and the cup of demons, child.

Abbessa Elena Fevronia

"There's a nun on our front porch," my little brother announced one October morning, "and she's so tall she could hunt geese with a rake."

She spoke with an accent that sounded vaguely familiar.
Menya zovut Abbessa Elena Fevronia. Vin pentru Nikanor.

According to my grandfather she had come all the way from Transylvania to reunite Nikanor with his real mother. My grandfather explained that Mila had already gotten the child last

winter. Twisting her rosary beads to the point of near shatter, she bellowed: *Neyt! neyt!* Apparently, Mila Khilkoff was Niki's nursemaid.

And then she asked to see the Romanov jewels and silver settings.

To say you could hear a pin drop, that my grandfather turned as white as her habit, that Abbessa Elena Fevronia didn't rage from our house with her tin

of lemon drops and loaf of *cozonac* still under her arm, would be a lie.

Well now, my grandfather sighed, taking out his pipe, *we can all stop squirming like a bunch of worms on hot brick, what's done is done—*

Where is that blueberry pie?

Mrs. Reed's Boarding House, South Bend

Huddled under my grandmother's quilt we listened to the pines echo, which Addison called the saddest sound in the whole world. Trying to talk her into staying was pointless, even though she and George had agreed to part ways.

But I want a normal life, children for heaven's sake and an upstanding man to take care of me.
There will never be another you love.

On the night she boarded the train for Osgood, I fell asleep at my desk, the smell of the paperwhites, the monarch soft kisses, Addy—

Whatever awaited me, I could not imagine.

Aunt Ida

She worked at the Singer Sewing Machine Factory in South Bend. My father said she knew her way around lumber, could veneer a black walnut cabinet faster than any man.

If she ever complained about the sixteen-hour shifts, it was to my grandfather's urn that sat atop the organ. On her days off, if she wasn't playing and singing hymns, she sat in the rocker with it

wrapped inside a faded bathrobe, which gave my mother the hives, especially when on the anniversary of his death, Ida draped a black tie over the urn and set it in the front window along

with a candle. After the Singer factory shut down, Ida started taking in feral cats. When there got to be so many, we lost count, she built a tiny cabin along the back fence and turned her house

over to the felines, who became so territorial, you couldn't get through the door without getting shanghaied. With the surplus of sewing machine cabinets, she'd acquired; she had transformed

her house into a menagerie of cat nooks and ceiling high trestles. She told us it gave the kitties boundaries, and those boundaries kept society from running amok—boundaries and plenty of fresh milk for the multitudes.

Let her be, said my father, and so we did. We left her in God's hands.

Ghost People

It wasn't the first time there'd been sightings.

Great Aunt Hannah's ghost often flickered in the milkweed where the outhouse had once stood, and twice Millicent saw her gossamer parents coming out of the chicken coup.

I can still smell the poultice of cat's claw and dandelion that appeared on the sideboard whenever one of us was sick.

But the day I discovered the ghosts of Billy and his mother down by the river, my heart leapt. I wanted to jump right in and swim across. I had missed them forever.

But then I heard Billy's voice in my mind, *Don't, we haven't been born yet.*

His mother glimpsing at something in the distance.

I blew him a kiss just as they began to fade. I heard Billy ask:

Mother, where is my kite?

Hubbard Squash

The summer my little brother's pig lost at the county fair, the Gilly cousins' squash tied for first place in the Indiana Gourd Society show.

It was a silent winning, no monkeys riding dogs, no horse pulls—Shires, or Belgians—but two puny blue ribbons set beside the squash and other gourd memorabilia.

Near the end of day, Millicent noticed a forlorn Fannie and Gert plopped beside their hubbards. When Millicent inquired, Gert exclaimed:

We are tired of squash. Whether it's a candy roaster, buttercup, hubbard or turban.
All we want to do by gosh, is to stop growing the winning squash!

"I don't blame you one bit," Millicent agreed, and told Oscar to load the girls and the whole kit and kaboodle into the wagon.

"Let's get some ice cream and cake before we take you home," Oscar said.
"Now that you're finished with squash, what is your secret?"

Goat's milk and a full moon.

Horace

He had just finished medical school when he came to visit me in South Bend. I'd sold a few of my short stories but the truth was, though I wouldn't admit it, working days at the county library

and nights waiting tables had run me ragged. Horace said it was time to call a spade a spade. *Look at you*, he said, *you're malnourished and pale as ashes.* And actually, I couldn't remember

the last time I'd had a square meal. Horace insisted we eat supper at the Oliver Hotel where I consumed an entire plate of roast pork with mashed potatoes and two pieces of pineapple

upside down cake. We were sipping our coffee when Horace took my hand and said he'd purchased a home in Osgood with a summer cottage which could easily be made into a doctor's

office. And in the main house, he said, was a room where I could write, with picture windows looking out over the orchard.

Let's get married—let's go home. By the way, here is a photo of one of the occupants.
Even squinting my eyes I tell you, that piglet was blowing me a kiss.

What else could I say, but yes.

Saffron and Sage

They could outrun any of us and had a knack for squeezing into the tightest hiding spots—abandoned muskrat burrows, for example. My grandmother called them little pills who someday would have to account for their sins.

Who would steal a day-old kitten from its mother? she'd ask.

What child knows how to pawn a ruby ring?

Their father doesn't know the difference between a boar and a gilt, my father complained, *I'll bet that weasel is running from the law.*

The day after the girls were caught stealing a pitchfork and four cigars, after having driven Manly Debeck's tractor into the creek, the whole family disappeared—

Good riddance, someone said, *how much maelstrom can two children cause?*

It was my grandmother who read the headline aloud that January morning: Boston Molasses Flood Kills Hundreds in Sea of Sticky Goo. Among the dead is an ex-farmer and his family from Osgood, Indiana.

When the foot slips, God's wrath pours in. Poor souls never saw it coming…

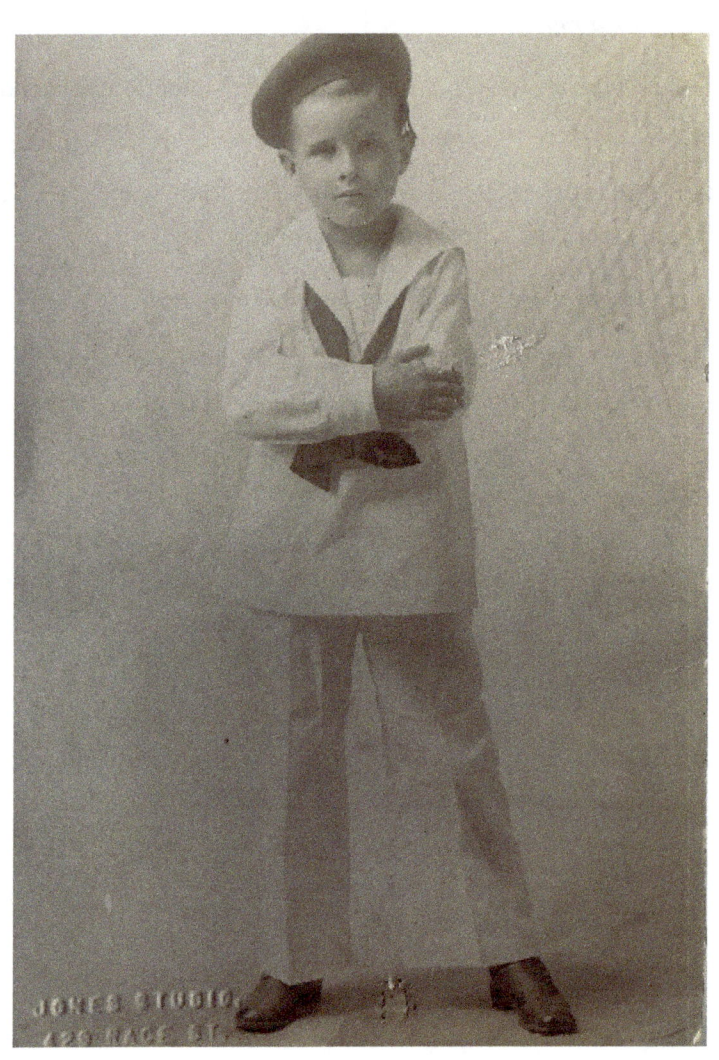

William Fading

It all started when his mother chose the sailor suit for his portrait
which William said was ridiculous because no kid in Osgood Indiana
went around in white blouses and britches let alone a scarf tied in a sissy bow.

Our teacher called William William the Conqueror until it got harder and harder
to see him. We all had theories as to what was causing his evaporation.

Mr. Bruner at the Rexall thought that because William's bowels were always
blocked up and that William was forced to take castor oil five times a day,
all that grease oozing through his pores was simmering William into oblivion.

One day I spied William coming out of the Livery and Feed holding a tin cup.
I followed his fuzzy sheen onto Buckeye Street and down the dirt road
that ended at Wilson's Dairy Farm. He disappeared inside the milk house

and that was the last time anyone ever saw William again.

Lena

In my great aunt Lena's diary there were notes, notes about things no one talked about. Notes my mother had no idea I had found in the root cellar and committed to memory:

Missionary position only. Keep legs flat.
Standing up or with knees drawn leads to cancer.

Over excitement leads to build up of nervous force, blindness, stroke, insanity.
Avoid.

Allow decent interval after meals before…
Once a month only, so organs can recover.

Alcohol loosens morals.
Refrain.

Lying down in bath will cause impure thoughts.
Wetting body all over causes infection.

Stand using cold sponge.

This explains a lot.

Arthur Doe

The fact that Arthur Doe was in his cups most days didn't seem to affect business.

His barber shop provided a hub of huddling, wheeling and dealing—a place to hobnob over cigars and brandy, not to mention argue about whose baseball team was the best.

I had my heart set on a bob haircut with marcel waves and asked Horace why on earth I was not allowed inside.

Because it is the domain of men, dear. You wouldn't think of walking down the street in a dressing gown carrying a bath sponge—

Would you?

I shook my head, dug a heel into the wood plank.

Concocted a plan.

Ours

They fought like cats and dogs and most nights ended up caboodled in the same bed. They ate faster than I could cook, even squash, even mincemeat pie. Their favorite game was hide

and seek and *accidentally* losing their tomboy sister, who only pretended to be lost. No matter how many times we lectured on kind versus unkind, it made no difference. Teasing and pulling

pranks was bred into them. *They didn't get that behavior from my side of the family,* Horace mused, and then much to our children's pleasure, I would remind him of the Tuffin sisters' Friday

night seances and all of the tomfoolery we had a hand in. And then the pleading would begin:

Tell us again about the fake skeleton—About the time father pretended to be the voice of Caroline's dead husband and she choked on her own spit, oh mother, tell us about the ghostly hand—

And the next morning at the foot of our bed under a single sheet, there would be an undulating three headed octopus:

We are your dead children from beyond the grave, bringing you news from the spirit world—

At the same time there was hooting and hollering and falling into our arms, I wanted to cry, for this moment had already boarded the train and there was nothing I could do to call it back.

Laddie

A dog is a dog is a dog, my father liked to say. And then there was Laddie. We found him when he was a pup one morning curled up asleep between two piglets.

He seemed to have come out of nowhere which was common for Osgood. He suckled with the other piggies and by the time he'd been weaned he knew his way around the farm like a pro.

That dog is more clever than Eleanor Webb's brother, Rufus, my father said. Laddie was someone you could tell your secrets, who understood when you were heartbroken over some childhood crush.

That cleverness needed to be passed on, according to my father, who borrowed Manly Debeck's spaniel, Mary-Queen-of-Scots, and left them to their own devices.

Two months later Mary delivered three pups that in the right sort of light, resembled a mishmash of pink—Maybe it was the ruby hue of their eyes or maybe it was nothing.

The genius of God, my father said, *the genius of God*

Hattie

Having been a former debutant, we assumed Hattie would marry well, as in high-class, as in biscuits, as in clams—move to Indianapolis, Cincinnati, New York—not marry the town soak, Arthur Doe.

My mother bemoaned how Hattie's mother would turn over in her grave, not only because Hattie wound up with a man like Arthur but also because Hattie had changed—from a demure, soft-spoken girl into a tobacco smoking, ribald crackerjack who for all intents and purposes, did as she pleased.

As a result, Arthur spent many nights sleeping curled up in the glider swing on the front porch because Hattie, as free thinking as she appeared, had no tolerance for drunkenness. *Arthur Doe do not be surprised if I leave you smack on your butt for someone who can appreciate and love me the way I deserve.* Needless to say it was Hattie I sought out regarding my hair dilemma.

Hattie, with a cigarette dangling from her lips, the latest issue of Harper's Bazaar tucked under one arm, and me on the other, marched into the shop, announcing to the stunned faces that in order to keep up with the times, from now on no woman wanting her hair cut, no matter how short, shall be turned away.

At the close of the next business day, Arthur flipped the "Come in We're Open" sign to "Sorry We're Closed," lead me in through the back door and chopped my locks into perfection.

Osgood is going straight to hell in a handbasket, my mother concluded, unaware that it was only the beginning.

Me

When they found me in the woods it was by the grace of God that Oscar's bullet had just missed my heart. Millicent was beside herself as they covered my body with maple leaves. *Oscar,*

why did you shoot that poor fox? I wasn't aiming for the fox, I thought it was a deer, he sighed. When I was certain they had gone, I shifted from fox back into myself. My grandfather had told

us stories about how shape shifting was passed down through generations, but because he said it was a sin, I never told that I could shift into anything I wanted, and had. Sometimes when

Addison fell asleep in the tree fort I shifted into the tree. From every bend and flexure, notch and nook, I embraced her. I shifted mostly into plants and animals because their souls were

at ease—the sugar pines, foxes, the gallop and sweat of horses. And in spring, the balsamic-blue notes of hyacinth. In a dream once, I asked my Great Aunt Hannah, why me—*For your*

poems, she mouthed, floating away. I have got to get out of Osgood before it's too late. But there is still the problem with my hair in bright sun, the leaf shadows fading in, fading out.

The Graveyard

I left the post office that day lark-happy, the envelope containing my contract with Harper's for five more stories would go out in the evening post. I stopped off to buy fresh strawberries—Horace and the children's favorite dessert, with cream of course, then took a shortcut home through the graveyard.

Ever since I was a child people thought my fondness for the place was morbid, *imagine* I can still hear myself saying, *all those poor souls roiling around in a void of nothing.* My grandfather was the one person who was positive that even the dead appreciated getting company.

When I got to our front gate, I was surprised to see my mother on the porch swing, snapping beans with my dog curled in her lap. *"Great St. Francis, protect all of God's creatures,"* I thought I heard her say before she faded into the clapboards.

Oh mother, don't let the children see you like this, or Horace for that matter. After all, you've been dead nine years.

Mr. and Mrs.

On Christmas Eve morning the announcement of Addison's engagement appeared underneath a snappy photograph in the society page of the Osgood Journal: "Miss Addison Eudora Hoyt of Osgood, Indiana to wed New York attorney John Emile Talbot, of Cleveland, Ohio.

The couple is planning a June wedding at the home of the groom's parents, Dr. and Mrs. Theodore Talbot. John Talbot is scheduled to join the New York law firm Cadwalader Wickersham & Taft on January first of next year."

This Talbot fellow sounds like a catch, Horace was saying, but I was already out the door down the steps, without coat or gloves, running as if Satan himself was at my heels, through the orchard, past the summer cottage, so rushed with tears I didn't see him rounding the corner and slammed full force only to collapse amidst a heavenly cloud of Fougère Royale.

There there n-n-now let's get you inside, Woolsey murmured, throwing his raccoon coat over my shoulders and offering his handkerchief. When I came out from freshening up, the side table had been set for tea and Manly, in his crimson smoking jacket and Egyptian shawl, patted the loveseat for me to join him.

Dearest one, you have got to return this agony to where it belongs... vaulted in the past.

And of course, he was horribly right. Even the piglet fussing in his lap and squealing, agreed, there was no choice—I let her go.

And then it was Christmas.

Abide

A handful of the farms remain.

The covered bridge on Laughery Creek, washed out during a cyclone that ended all cyclones.

The Jack pines are paved over, for better or worse. The wind is silent now.

But the family home on Buckeye Street, stands. The depot, library, Rexall
the Methodist and the Baptist churches, stand.

Our school on Society and Monroe, razed. But not The Academy.

On this side of the veil, what my mother thought was heaven, is only a different way
of seeing.

We pass each other and nod, pass each other and nod—

All of their photographs are ghosts. Even Laddie. Even me.

My Mother

After she died, she appeared in dreams, mostly to give advice. Occasionally to bear gifts, such as the pearl earrings left under my pillow the morning Horace and I were to be married.

The fact that they appeared today of all days, Millicent said at the time, was due to the *fancy footwork of ghosts.* O Osgood. O death.

I wasn't afraid, because my mother had told me years ago that whenever it came, *they* would all be there to collect me.

And they were—When my eyes adjusted—You could not begin to fathom it.

About the Author

Deborah Allbritain is a poet living in San Diego. Deborah's work has appeared in *The Baltimore Review, Barrow Steet, Beloit Poetry Journal, Ecotone, fugue, Salamander, Thrush,* and *Plume*. Individual poems have been finalists in the *Crab Creek Review* Poetry Prize, the *Wabash Poetry Prize*, the *Bellingham Review*'s Award for Poetry, the *Florida Review* Editors' Award, and the *Comstock Review* Poetry Contest. She received the Patricia Dobler Poetry Prize in 2017. Visit the author's website at https://willaflora.com.

Our Mission

The mission of Brick Road Poetry Press is to publish and promote poetry that entertains, amuses, edifies, and surprises a wide audience of appreciative readers. We are not qualified to judge who deserves to be published, so we concentrate on publishing what we enjoy. Our preference is for poetry geared toward dramatizing the human experience in language rich with sensory image and metaphor, recognizing that poetry can be, at one and the same time, both familiar as the perspiration of daily labor and as outrageous as a carnival sideshow.

Available from Brick Road Poetry Press

www.brickroadpoetrypress.com

All These Hungers by Rick Mulkey

Escape Envy by Ace Boggess

My Father Should Die in Winter by Barry Marks

The Return of the Naked Man by Robert Tremmel

Thrash by Michael Diebert

Face Cut Out For Locket by Jenn Blair

Natural Violence by Jennifer Brown

Miracle Strip by Matthew Layne

Reading Szymborska in a Time of Plague by Joan Baranow

First Time, Every Time by Lisa Titus

Osgood by Deborah Allbritain

A Brief Campaign of Sting and Sweet by Laura Amsel

Available from Brick Road Poetry Press

www.brickroadpoetrypress.com

The Word in Edgewise by Sean M. Conrey

Household Inventory by Connie Jordan Green

Practice by Richard M. Berlin

A Meal Like That by Albert Garcia

Cracker Sonnets by Amy Wright

Things Seen by Joseph Stanton

Battle Sleep by Shannon Tate Jonas

Lauren Bacall Shares a Limousine by Susan J. Erickson

Ambushing Water by Danielle Hanson

Having and Keeping by David Watts

Assisted Living by Erin Murphy

Credo by Steve McDonald

The Deer's Bandanna by David Oates

Creation Story by Steven Owen Shields

Touring the Shadow Factory by Gary Stein

American Mythology by Raphael Kosek

Waxing the Dents by Daniel Edward Moore

Speaking Parts by Beth Ruscio

Also Available from Brick Road Poetry Press

www.brickroadpoetrypress.com

Dancing on the Rim by Clela Reed

Possible Crocodiles by Barry Marks

Pain Diary by Joseph D. Reich

Otherness by M. Ayodele Heath

Drunken Robins by David Oates

Damnatio Memoriae by Michael Meyerhofer

Lotus Buffet by Rupert Fike

The Melancholy MBA by Richard Donnelly

Two-Star General by Grey Held

Chosen by Toni Thomas

Etch and Blur by Jamie Thomas

Water-Rites by Ann E. Michael

Bad Behavior by Michael Steffen

Tracing the Lines by Susanna Lang

Rising to the Rim by Carol Tyx

Treading Water with God by Veronica Badowski

Rich Man's Son by Ron Self

Just Drive by Robert Cooperman

The Alp at the End of My Street by Gary Leising

About the Prize

The Brick Road Poetry Prize, established in 2010, is awarded annually for the best book-length poetry manuscript. Entries are accepted August 1st through November 1st. The winner receives $1000 and publication. For details on our preferences and the complete submission guidelines, please visit our website at www.brickroadpoetrypress.com.

Winners of the Brick Road Poetry Prize

2022
A Brief Campaign of Sting and Sweet by Laura Amsel

2021
Reading Szymborska in a Time of Plague by Joan Baranow

2019
Return of the Naked Man by Robert Tremmel

2018
Speaking Parts by Beth Ruscio

2017
Touring the Shadow Factory by Gary Stein

2016
Assisted Living by Erin Murphy

2015
Lauren Bacall Shares a Limousine by Susan J. Erickson

2014
Battle Sleep by Shannon Tate Jonas

2013
Household Inventory by Connie Jordan Green

2012
The Alp at the End of My Street by Gary Leising

2011
Bad Behavior by Michael Steffen

2010
Damnatio Memoriae by Michael Meyerhofer

www.ingramcontent.com/pod-product-compliance
Lightning Source LLC
Chambersburg PA
CBHW080639170426
43200CB00015B/2899